Don't Call Me
DUMB

Dr. Noah Johnson

ISBN 13: **978-1-945532-06-1**

Published, Cover Illustration & Edited by
Opportune Independent Publishing Company

Printed in the United States of America

For permission requests, write to the publisher, addressed "Attention: Permissions Coordinator" to the address below.

info@opportunepublishing.com
www. opportunepublishing.com

CHAPTER 1

You Can Be
Anything You Want
To Be

Infancy to early childhood is a time when people thrive and soar most in life. Why? Could it be because of how they feel about life at that time? Unconditional positive speaking and reinforcement is the first language in every household. Parents, grandparents, siblings, family and friends all issue the same type of communication. They shower them with words like:

• You can be anything you want to be
• You are amazing
• You are beautiful
• You are handsome

- You are the best
- Shoot for the stars
- I will never allow anything to hurt you
- You're safe
- You're a king/queen
- You're a prince/princess.

When children hear positive affirmations it seems to echo with each word. What else are they to believe? Just think about it... when a child is learning to walk they hear, "Come on, you can do it." Infants are showered with an unlimited amount of positive reinforcements, because our next statement is, "DO IT AGAIN". Therefore initiating a repeat of the toddlers' attempt to walk. Watch this − No matter what happens during the repeat. You will hear come on, you can do it................... I am glad I was a recipient of this type of love.

Life presents us with many challenges. One of life's most important challenges is education. From elementary, middle school, high school, and even college, we are at war with many educational trials, test, and battles. Everyone faces the challenges differently. Some fail − You may be at the point where you fail a test, a grade level, two, or three grade levels. You ask the question," I have failed, what do I do, now?" Some decide to quit and give up. They make statements like, "I just can't get it", "I just don't understand, am I dumb", "my brain doesn't work right"," I am special", "My teacher said I won't make it, "my teacher called me stupid." Does any of this sound familiar? Maybe, some of you have heard this or your children are going through this right now. The teacher says, if your child's behavior was better, they could learn. Parents and children, "Do Not Give Up" I have found during my research there are some teachers out there who tells students what they can and can't do, instead of encouraging those students to do things right and allowing them to build on that. Each parent, teacher, and student has a responsibility for education. Parents take responsibility for your child's education.

Students take responsibility for your own education. Don't settle for less don't short change yourself.

ATTITUDES, STRESS, AND ANXIETY IN EDUCATION TODAY PRESCHOOL TO COLLEGE

Stress is a normal part of life. From birth to death, a person endures stress. Although impossible, it is not always a great idea to actually avoid the stresses in life. Stress is a perceived concept, meaning that it can be caused by anything that one feels unbalances the harmony in his or her life. Stress is defined in many ways. According to Neuman, a stressor is any relationship between the person and the environment that is appraised by the person taxing. The relationship can result in either a beneficial or a harmful ending. Because there is an array of stresses, the result or effect can be vary, depending on the situation and individual. Some people will suffer from anxiety, which results in feelings of apprehension that can ultimately lead to negative emotional, physical, cognitive and behavioral symptoms.

The process of encountering increasing and changing amounts of stress over a period of time helps one to develop methods of stress management in adulthood. There are several things one can do to assist with adaptation: exercise, spend time with friends, relax and participate in endeavors that improve self-concept.

The research by Roth and Cohen (1986) on coping identified two basic orientations to stress - approach and avoidance refers to the cognitive and emotional activity that is oriented either to or away from a threat. Approach strategies refer to attempting to take appropriate action to either change a situation or to make it more controllable. On the other hand, avoidance strategies attempt to protect the individual from the overwhelming power of the stressor by distancing the individual from the experience.

Research has shown that when students perceive stress as being a negative thing, or it becomes excessive, they experience physical and psychological impairments. This is obviously a serious issue that can affect other areas of their life, so it is recommended that students often include effective time management, social support, positive reappraisal, and engagement in leisure pursuits. Leisure satisfaction is defined as a positive feeling of contentment one perceives as a result of meeting personal needs through leisure activities (Seigenthaler, 19997).

Strenuous academic pressure and limited social and personal time can add to the normal stress of life and begin to have a negative affect on students. In a perfect world, it would be easy to separate stresses that come from certain places in order to prioritize academia and socializing. Daily stressors in life cannot be avoided, nor can major life changes. Stressful events that change one's life for and extended period can lead to health related problems. Events that may cause unhealthy stress include death, divorce, moving away form home, serious illness, and financial struggles. These are all normal things in life that can occur, but some cope differently with such major events. Those who dwell on life events suffer with higher stress throughout life.

For preschool children, learning is fun. There usually aren't any motivational problems for learning during these years. Their motivation is manifested by their choice, intensity, latency and persistence of behavior, and is accompanied with cognitive and emotional reactions. Motivation is often considered to be a necessary prerequisite and partner for learning. Continuing motivation is the antecedent to learning more; a person will retain the positive reinforcement for learning and use that to acquire new and additional knowledge on their own going forward. Children's abilities to form and maintain styles and strategies of coping with the social environment in early school years are important factors in establishing a trajectory of academic and behavioral performance (Entwisle & Hayduk, 1988; Lynch & Cicchetti, 1997; Pianta, Steinberg, & Rollins, 1995). The teacher-student relationship, even early in a child's school career, can cause later problems and successes. Although, from the teachers' perspective, strong, positive relationships with students can provide motivation to spend extra time and energy promoting their success. In contrast, other teacher-student relationships characterized by conflict may lead to frequent attempts to control children's behavior and thus hinder efforts to promote a positive school environment for them. This may be one of the reasons why negative teacher-child relationships are related to efforts to exclude certain children from the classroom. However, there is a certain balance that should be made in order to avoid other issues for the children being so attached to their teachers. For example, high levels of child dependence on the teacher has been correlated with school adjustment difficulties, including more negative school attitudes and less positive engagement with the school environment. Excessively dependent children are also more likely to be socially withdrawn and aggressive with peers (Howes et al., 1994) Children at risk of school failure may have the most to gain, or lose, through their ability to adapt to the social environment of the classroom. Therefore, it was expected that the association between early teacher- child relationships and later school performance would be strongest for those children with low verbal abilities, and or children with significant early behavioral problems would be predicted by kindergarten teachers' ratings of relationship quality.

The topic of stress among college or university students has been a subject of much research for many years. Researchers have found that the perception of high stress levels in student can lead to poor academic performance, depression and serious health problems. Therefore, the study of this phenomenon and how students deal with it can have important implications for higher education administrators.

College students experience high stress at predictable times each semester due to academic commitments, financial pressures, and lack of time management skills. When is stress perceived negatively or becomes excessive, it can affect students in multiple areas, particularly with health and academic performance. University students often attempt to control and reduce their stress through avoidance, religious and social support, or fitness activities. Stress is also reduced and controlled through effective time management and study techniques for some. A Study found that students who perceived themselves in control of their time reported greater work and life satisfactions. Which also meant that job-induced and somatic tensions were decreased.

A few studies have examined faculty perceptions of students' behaviors. This is something we take for granted, or never fully examine, but it can play a major role in the attitudes and success of students. Studies indicate that student behavior is linked to attitudes of faculty members. Faculty from predominantly teaching - or research oriented universities, however, differ in how they evaluate students' behavior. (Brozo &

Schmelzer, 1985). Interaction with the students significantly influences faculty behaviors as well. Stress levels of faculty members vary due to personal and organizational behaviors that may affect their interactions with students. Although stress-causing stimuli are often similar in the lives of professors and students, teachers also bring stress into the classroom in the form of inherent personality traits. However, the stressful personality of a teacher may sometimes be perceived as a positive, rather than a negative, attribute by students. It is vital for faculty members to have an accurate perception of students' academic stresses in order to have effective communication with them. For instance faculty may highly prioritize prompt attendance and good academic performance, while some students may not necessarily value such items. While instead they hold actual knowledge acquired higher up on the totem pole.

CHAPTER 2

························

Power of
Intrinsic and Extrinsic
Factors in Education

Intrinsic Factors

Intrinsic motivation is defined as the doing of an activity for its inherent satisfactions rather than for some separable consequence. When intrinsically motivated, a person is moved to act for the fun or challenge entailed rather than because of external prods, pressures, or rewards. The phenomenon of intrinsic motivation was first acknowledged within experimental studies of animal behavior, where it was discovered that many organisms engage in exploratory, playful, and curiosity-driven behaviors even in the absence of reinforcement or reward. These spontaneous behaviors, although clearly bestowing adaptive benefits on the organism, appear no to be associated with exercising and extending ones capacities.

There are many different perspectives on the components of intrinsic motivation and this may be because it is contextual in that it varies over time, circumstances, and how people view what they are doing. This theory posits that people are innately motivated to seek out optimal stimulation and challenges that meet the needs of autonomy, competence, and relatedness. Autonomy need is the need of humans to feel that they are in control of their environment and is similar to the control in the flow theory that will be discussed later. That is, environments that provide choices and self-direction support the feeling of autonomy, which enhances intrinsic motivation. Competence need is the need to feel capable of acting appropriately in an environment and is similar to the matching of skills to challenge in flow theory. Relatedness is the need to feel secure and connected to others in the learning environment, particularly to the teachers and other authority figures. The need for security and connectedness is closely aligned with Maslow's(1955) theory of hierarchy of human needs for affectionate relationships and the feeling of being part of a group. In support of the existence of the belongingness need, there have numerous studies demonstrating that cooperative learning and group activities, such as those provided in problem-based learning environments have a positive effect on students' interest, engagement, and motivation. There is a huge desire of individuals to establish, strengthen, and maintain interpersonal relations - the sense of belonging to and participating in a social group or community. When researchers express their views of intrinsic motivation the diversity of interest varies, as summarized below:

Humans as problem solvers: challenge, competence, efficacy or mastery.

(Researchers- Bandura, Deci, Harter, Lepper, Weiner, and White)

Humans as information processors: curiosity, incongruity, or discrepancy.

(Researchers- Berlyne, Hunt, Kagan, and Piaget)

Humans as voluntary actors: control and self-determination.

(Researchers- Condry, DeCharms, Deci, Nuttin, and Ryan)

Extrinsic Factors is a construct that pertains whenever an activity is done in order to attain some separable outcome. Extrinsic motivation thus contrasts with intrinsic motivation, which refers to doing an activity simply for the enjoyment of the activity itself, rather than its instrumental value. However, unlike some perspectives that view extrinsically motivated behavior as invariantly non-autonomous, SDT proposes that extrinsic motivation can vary greatly in the degree to which it is autonomous. For example, a student who does his homework only because he fears parental sanctions for not doing it is extrinsically motivated because he is doing the work in order to attain the separable outcome of avoiding sanctions. Similarly, a student who does work because he personally believes it is valuable for her chosen career is also extrinsically motivated because she too is doing it for its instrumental value rather because she finds it interesting. Both examples involve instrumentalities, yet the latter case entails personal endorsement and a feeling of choice, whereas the former involves mere compliance with an external control. Both represent intentional behavior, but the two types of extrinsic motivation vary in their relative autonomy.

Given that many of the educational activities prescribed in schools are not designed to be intrinsically interesting, a central question concerns how to motivate students to value and self-regulate such activities, and without external pressure, to carry them out on their own. This problem is described within SDT in terms of fostering of fostering the internalization and integration of values and behavior regulations

CHAPTER 3

I Failed, What do I do now?
Success is Possible
I Will Never Give Up

Stress Reduction and Test Taking Methods Prescriptions have been written for years by hypnotist around the world to aid in working with people who have difficulty passing exams due to stress. Dr. E. Arthur Winkler, Th.D. ,Ph.D. who has induced over 30,000 people wrote the following prescription used in this study. The students simply had to play the individualized CD given to them at night while they were asleep placing the CD player on repeat. The words were written by Dr. Winkler, the music by Dr. C. Adam's Sea of Infinity, and words spoken by the principle investor in this study. Close your eyes… just relax and take a deep breath. You have been responding good to the suggestions and recommendations I've been telling you… You can continue responding to the instructions I tell you and you will be able to pass all tests and exams you take from now on...

These suggestions are very important, and will have the effects of helping you during your future life... Because of the benefit these suggestions will be to you, your inner mind is accepting them all and will cause you to put them into your own actions... From now on, any time you are going to take a test, or examination, or even a quiz, the moment you pick up a pen or pencil to answer the question... You will immediately become calm, relaxed and peaceful, the way you are right now... You will be able to keep your eyes open... you will be able to read the questions... The normal conditions of your surroundings will be perfectly suited for you to take the test, or examination, or quiz, and answer the questions correctly... You will be able to concentrate on the test, or examination, or quiz ten time better than you ever have before...

In addition to the improved ability to concentrate, you will be able to recall everything you have read and studied to answer the questions correctly... You will recall everything you need to remember to pass the test, or examination, or quiz with a high score... Your concentration will be so good that you will be able to answer the questions rapidly... After completing the test, or exam, or quiz, you will be wide awake, fully alert and you will feel confident that you have been successful in answering the questions correctly...

Whatever amount of tests, or examinations, or quizzes you take, you will always become calm and relaxed the moment you pick up the pen or pencil to answer the questions... You will always have the wonderful ability to recall the answers clearly and easily...

You now understand what I have told you, and your unconscious mind will cause you to follow my suggestions automatically from now on for the rest of your life. Now close your eyes and say out loud the work, able...(Pause.)

That good... Now notice that your eyelids feel as though they are sealed shut... Test them to be sure they remain shut... You will notice that your in the same relaxed state you were in when I hypnotized you...

Now say the second word, study, and open your eyes.... Now say the third word, better... Notice that you can move freely... now if you want to stay in this state will say all three words together; able, study, better, and you will remain in this relaxed, intensive studying state for thirty minutes...

You have done excellent... Now count to five slowly and bring yourself out of the hypnotic state... Then I want you to go through the entire procedure again, following my instructions... And finally I will have you go through the procedure yourself... (Note: Have the student go through the entire procedure several times to be sure it is understood.)

Dr. Winkler's words are strategically placed to be delivered directly to the subconscious mind of the participants. Bypassing the critical factory of the conscious mind. Psychologist have argued for years that it takes about 21 days to completely change a habit, but none divulge immediate documented changes, unless the individual was in crisis. When Dr. Winkler used the words able, learn, and better the conscious mind heard just that able, learn, better, but the subconscious mind heard (I AM ABLE TO LEARN BETTER). This series is repeated for and individual who receives about 8 hours of sleep a night 480 minutes about 21.82 times a night times 60 days for 1309.09 times hearing (I AM ABLE TO LEARN BETTER). The music works as a positive distracter for the conscious mind. Which allows the words to help pass the critical faculty of the conscious mind.

The results of this study indicate that familial factors such as parental academic desires for their children and parental educational attainment have an impact on student academic desires and

23

intentions, which suggest that education-related intrinsic factors are mostly fostered from home. In addition, although there is a lot of variability with regard to students' attitudes towards school and their study habits, the majority of those surveyed in this study had positive attitudes toward school and study by them self in a quiet place. However, those surveyed in this study are not likely to study more than one hour a day; although they are not likely to wait until the night or day of a test to study.

With regard to the impact of the techniques used in the 30-day challenge, the results of this study indicate that they can help to reduce stress, reduce anxiety associated with test taking and improve students' grades. Therefore hypnosis appears to be a modality that can be used for positive extrinsic reinforcement. Also, the fact that students who completed the 30-day challenge were more likely to have improved grades suggests that if students take the proper actions, they can matriculate at the university level. Finally, students are most likely to begin taking these actions around sophomore or junior year, according to the results of this study.

Finally, the fact that the students in this study who were part of the 30-day challenge tended to have positive academic motivation suggests that hypnosis may have been able to help participants change negative influences in their environment to positive messages. However, the data from this study do not allow for a cause and effect determination, but simply indicate that those who participated in the 30-day challenge had more positive than negative academic motivation scores.

. . . .

To be a

Better & Smarter

Me

Day 1

Affirmation: Today is my new start. I am getting better and better in every way.

- ➤ Items you will need one book of your choice about 130 to 150 pages to read.
- ➤ One Notebook to take notes or write words you may not know
- ➤ One Dictionary or Smart Phone with Internet Access

Assignment: Read the first 5 pages, then turn to the Reflections section Day 1. Write 5 sentences about what you just read. This will take about one hour...

Great job! You have completed your assignment for today. I am so proud of you. It is time to reward yourself.

Day 2

Affirmation: I am getting smarter and smarter every day in every way.

Assignment: Read the next 5 pages, now read your reflection from day 1, then write your reflection for day 2. You will find you remembered ALL the key parts of what you have read this for.

Great job! You have completed your assignment for today. Begin looking forward to reading tomorrow. Reward yourself you deserve it.

Day 3

Affirmation: I am happy and excited, because I am getting better and better everyday.

Assignment: Read the next 5 pages, now read your reflection from day 2, then write your reflection for day 3. You will find you remembered ALL the key parts of what you have read this for.

Awesome! You are amazing. You have completed your assignment for today. You are well on your way to success. Reward yourself you deserve it.

Day 4

Affirmation: Today my memory is stronger and I can remember everything I read.

Assignment: Read the next 5 pages, now read your reflection from day 3, then write your reflection for day 4. You will find you remembered ALL the key parts of what you have read this for.

Magnificent! You are a winner. You have completed your assignment for today. You are successful. Reward yourself you are amazing.

Day 5

Affirmation: I can remember everything that I read. My future is getting brighter and brighter.

Assignment: Read the next 5 pages, now read your reflection from day 4, then write your reflection for day 5. You will find you remembered ALL the key parts of what you have read this for.

Great job! You are making progress. You should be getting a feeling like you want to do more. I am so excited for you. Don't forget to reward yourself.

Day 6

Affirmation: I am smart, when I read today I will remember everything.

Assignment: Read the next 5 pages, now read your reflection from day 5, then write your reflection for day 6. You will find you remembered ALL the key parts of what you have read this for.

Amazing job! You are better today, then yesterday. I am very proud of you. It's reward time.

Day 7

Affirmation: What I have to say matters, I am getting better and better and my memory is perfect.

Assignment: Read the next 5 pages, now read your reflection from day 6, then write your reflection for day 7. You will find you remembered ALL the key parts of what you have read this for.

Awesome! You have completed your assignment for today. Feel the excitement, you just can't wait until tomorrow. You are well on your way to success. Reward yourself you deserve it.

Day 8

Affirmation: Today is a great day for learning. I can't wait to read today.

Assignment: Read the next 5 pages, now read your reflection from day 7, then write your reflection for day 8. You will find you remembered ALL the key parts of what you have read this for.

Awesome! You are amazing. You have completed your assignment for today. You are well on your way to success. Reward yourself you deserve it.

Day 9

Affirmation: *I am happy and excited, because I am getting better and better everyday*

Assignment: Read the next 5 pages, now read your reflection from day 8, then write your reflection for day 9. You will find you remembered ALL the key parts of what you have read this for.

Great job! You have completed your assignment for today. You should be proud of yourself. It is time to reward yourself.

Day 10

Affirmation: When I read today I will remember everything. My memory is perfect.

Assignment: Read the next 5 pages, now read your reflection from day 9, then write your reflection for day 10. You will find you remembered ALL the key parts of what you have read this for.

Amazing! You have completed your assignment for today. I know you can't wait for the next one. It is time to reward yourself.

Day 11

Affirmation: When I read today I will remember everything. My memory is perfect. I am getting better and better every day in every way.

Assignment: Read the next 5 pages, now read your reflection from day 10, then write your reflection for day 11. You will find you remembered ALL the key parts of what you have read this for.

Amazing job! You are better today, then yesterday. I am very proud of you. It's reward time.

Day 12

Affirmation: I am happy and learning. When I read today I will remember everything. My memory is perfect.

Assignment: Read the next 5 pages, now read your reflection from day 11, then write your reflection for day 12. You will find you remembered ALL the key parts of what you have read this for.

Delightful! You are better today, then yesterday. I am very proud of you. It's reward time.

Day 13

Affirmation: Today is the perfect day to use my perfect memory. When I read today I will remember everything. My memory is perfect.

Assignment: Read the next 5 pages, now read your reflection from day 12, then write your reflection for day 13. You will find you remembered ALL the key parts of what you have read this for.

Job well done! You are better today, then yesterday. I am very proud of you. It's reward time.

Day 14

Affirmation: I love my perfect memory. I am reading today just for fun, and I remember everything. My memory is perfect.

Assignment: Read the next 5 pages, now read your reflection from day 13, then write your reflection for day 14. You will find you remembered ALL the key parts of what you have read this for.

That's fantastic! You are better today, then yesterday. I am very proud of you. It's reward time.

Day 15

Affirmation: When I read today I will remember everything. My memory is perfect. Test me I know the information.

Assignment: Read the next 5 pages, now read your reflection from day 14, then write your reflection for day 15. You will find you remembered ALL the key parts of what you have read this for.

You're the best! You are better today, then yesterday. I am very proud of you. It's reward time.

Day 16

Affirmation: Today is my day, every day is getting brighter and brighter. Perfect memory just for me.

Assignment: Read the next 5 pages, now read your reflection from day 15, then write your reflection for day 16. You will find you remembered ALL the key parts of what you have read this for.

Terrific! You are better today, then yesterday. I am very proud of you. It's reward time.

Day 17

Affirmation: Reading is fun. I can have fun reading every day. Perfect memory just for me.

Assignment: Read the next 5 pages, now read your reflection from day 16, then write your reflection for day 17. You will find you remembered ALL the key parts of what you have read this for.

Wonderful! You are better today, then yesterday. I am very proud of you. It's reward time.

Day 18

Affirmation: Today I am going to read faster, and still have perfect memory.

Assignment: Read the next 5 pages, now read your reflection from day 17, then write your reflection for day 18. You will find you remembered ALL the key parts of what you have read this for.

Well done! You are better today, then yesterday. I am very proud of you. It's reward time.

Day 19

Affirmation: I can pass any test, just let me read the material. I have perfect memory.

Assignment: Read the next 5 pages, now read your reflection from day 18, then write your reflection for day 19. You will find you remembered ALL the key parts of what you have read this for.

Super Job! You are better today, then yesterday. I am very proud of you. It's reward time.

Day 20

Affirmation: I have an amazing memory, I look forward to taking test.

Assignment: Read the next 5 pages, now read your reflection from day 19, then write your reflection for day 20. You will find you remembered ALL the key parts of what you have read this for.

Brilliant job! You are better today, then yesterday. I am very proud of you. What is your reward today?

Day 21

Affirmation: I believe in myself, even if no one else does. I am a force of strength.

Assignment: Read the next 5 pages, now read your reflection from day 20, then write your reflection for day 21. You will find you remembered ALL the key parts of what you have read this for.

I believe in myself! You have completed your assignment for today just for me. You are well on your way to success. Reward yourself you deserve it.

Day 22

Affirmation: I can do this, watch me.

Assignment: Read the next 5 pages, now read your reflection from day 21, then write your reflection for day 22. You will find you remembered ALL the key parts of what you have read this for.

You're the best, Awesome, and Amazing! You are better today, then yesterday. Be proud of yourself. It's reward time.

Day 23

Affirmation: I am doing this, I am powerful and strong.

Assignment: Read the next 5 pages, now read your reflection from day 22, then write your reflection for day 23. You will find you remembered ALL the key parts of what you have read this for.

I am champion material! You are better today, then yesterday. I am very proud of you. It's reward time.

Day 24

Affirmation: I am getting stronger and stronger. Can you see the smile on my face?

Assignment: Read the next 5 pages, now read your reflection from day 23, then write your reflection for day 24. You will find you remembered ALL the key parts of what you have read this for.

Nothing can hold you back! You define success. I am very proud of you. It's reward time. Great job!

Day 25

Affirmation: Reading comes easy and my memory is perfect. Check my scores as they go UP.

Assignment: Read the next 5 pages, now read your reflection from day 24, then write your reflection for day 25. You will find you remembered ALL the key parts of what you have read this for.

Great! You are smarter, then yesterday. I am very proud of you. It's reward time.

Day 26

Affirmation: I am worth it, reading makes it possible. A whole new world of opportunity.

Assignment: Read the next 5 pages, now read your reflection from day 25, then write your reflection for day 26. You will find you remembered ALL the key parts of what you have read this for.

You made the grade! You completed your task today. I am very proud of you. It's reward time.

Day 27

Affirmation: Today I am shooting for the stars, watch me soar.

Assignment: Read the next 5 pages, now read your reflection from day 26, then write your reflection for day 27. You will find you remembered ALL the key parts of what you have read this for.

You determine your destiny. Great job! You have completed your task today. What will your reward be today.

Day 28

Affirmation: I can and I will. Today is my day. I am getting better in every way.

Assignment: Read the next 5 pages, now read your reflection from day 27, then write your reflection for day 28. You will find you remembered ALL the key parts of what you have read this for.

Terrific job! I am very proud of you. You have learned to push, push, push, and push some more. It's reward time.

Day 29

Affirmation: I am healed, whole, and healthy. I have perfect memory.

Assignment: Read the next 5 pages, now read your reflection from day 28, then write your reflection for day 29. You will find you remembered ALL the key parts of what you have read this for.

Amazing! You have completed your assignment for today. I know you can't wait for your last assignment. It is time to reward yourself.

Day 30

Affirmation: I have let go of all the lies that I have been telling myself about my ability. I am smart, and strong.

Assignment: Read the next 5 pages, now read your reflection from day 29, then write your reflection for day 30. You will find you remembered ALL the key parts of what you have read this for.

You are complete. You have just read two books.

CONGRATULATIONS... You did it. You broke the chain. Great job! I am so proud of you and your accomplishment. You have done an amazing job. Today make sure your reward is BIG. Again, congratulations.

Faculty Moments On Education

As a youth I was once told, "If you want to hide something from a man, put it in a book." The treasure of our nation's future, even the world's future, will be found in the maximized potential of each citizen. Yet, many of our the world's citizenry have found neither the treasures of life nor the value of self as the result of an inability to read and comprehend the literature and language that frame the contexts of their lives. Their best is hidden within the pages of books they have not read.

As a nurse and educator, I regularly engage students who have great desires to change lives and positively impact the communities, and world, in which they find themselves. Many of these students face an insidious challenge developed over a period of years amidst a plethora of known and unknown challenges--they are unable to commit themselves to unlocking the hidden treasures to be found within texts foundational to their learning.

Dr. Johnson's book provides a practical tool and resource to support students, potential innovators, even the stewards of our future in their endeavors to change the world--to reveal the hidden treasures and maximized potential to be found in every individual and civilization.

It has been said, "Reading is fundamental." The aims of and opportunities provided by this book will prove fundamental to the success of each of its readers and the future of our treasured global community.

Dr. Marcus M. Gaut, RN
Faith Community Nurse | Assistant Professor

From my experience as a college professor, I have encountered numerous students in higher education who are unprepared. Many cannot read or write, but it is handed off by the university as a learning disability. I have encountered these students on a graduate level and often wondered, "Who read their admissions statement? Who interviewed them? And Who gave them false hope as they struggle to keep up?" We don't want to admit it, but the educational system failed these students years ago and somehow, they slipped through the cracks. When they arrive on these college campuses it becomes a matter of economics and they are allowed to continue their studies in settings that are not beneficial to them. At some point it becomes the job of their college professors to help them to play catch up and try and understand a mission that has become extremely impossible.

Dr. Carey D. Yazeed
Licensed Clinical Social Worker

The Heart of a Mother

Some schools, they counted you out, But My God, he counted you in. They said you couldn't finish, but you finished to the end. Some said you wouldn't make it, and dreams, you can never achieve, but we serve an awesome God. So, whose report will you believe? Sometimes along the road it was filled with hurt and pain but every time you fell, I dust you off and we started again. Sometimes I made mistakes, and forgive me when I do, but one mistake I'll never make, and that's giving up on you! CONGRATS MY SON! Your father and mother loves you!!!

Monique Wright-Edwards

Because I have been on both sides of the spectrum as a parent first of children who have been labeled with learning disabilities, as well as a substitute teacher in both the middle and high school sectors, I find that reading has become one of the fundamental resources that is not very relevant in normal school settings.

It has been my experience that smaller classes and inclusion, as well as private schools tend to focus more on reading and comprehension. A lot of students are simply passed along for the sake of getting them through the system.

It is my opinion that more focus needs to be placed on reading to secure learning and comprehension, not just reading words with no understanding, just enough to skate by.

There was a 17-year-old 8th grader in one of my classes at Middle School, who had been passed along continuously. I took a major interest in her deficiencies, and went above and beyond the call of duty to get her the type of assistance needed.

Once getting her some reading help with a tutor, moved to smaller classes, and actually implementing a process to assist her with her learning style, she flourished. Her name was Samantha, and she was able to not only get on, and stay on task, but she was also able to be promoted to her proper grade, and graduate on time.

This is proof that taking the time to completely educate, and not just pass along, is what constitutes being the major attribute to the success of the student.

Jamie L. Douglas-Edwards, MS

The importance of proficient reading and obtaining a quality education

My mother would always tell me "Knowledge is Power, and what you don't know can kill you." I have one son, according to me, I believed that it is very important my son know how to read and comprehend whatever it is he would read. I started reading to my son when I was pregnant with him, and I still find myself reading to him now that he is 16 years old and a senior in high school. A great reader starts at home with the parents / guardians encouraging / enforcing good reading habits daily with their child or children. Reading / comprehending are learned skills that cannot be taken away once learned. As a parent I realized early on that what one does not know will hurt them. When my son was a toddler I would not buy him action figures or toys, I would buy him books and educational games things what would stimulate his mind. I would read to him every night; and after reading to him for a certain period of time he was about to read the same books back to me. The impact of him being able to read back to me was so profound to me; I started to devote even more time reading with him instead of just at bed time. Once it was time for him to start pre-school he was much more advanced than some of his classmates why because it all started at home.

Throughout my son's school years I have been devoted to making sure he receives a quality education. Although, we have moved from state-to-state, and he have attended many schools I had to be mentally and physically involved in the quality of his schooling so that he was able to maintain due to the constant change. I felt it was mandatory for me to volunteer every week at the school in his classroom. I would take him to the park every day to play but, before he would be allowed to play we would go to the Library check-out a book. Then, we would read out loud to each other on the playground before he could go play. I would take him on the weekends to the mall to Barnes &Noble book store we would sit in the café to read, and as an incentive I would treat him to his favorite muffin and milk. As he grew older I had to start thinking of more creative ways to keep his attention when it came to reading and his schooling.

Once my son reached the 4th grade I could now longer use the tools I once used prior in the years. So, I had to turn to outside help in order to keep reinforcing including stressing to him how important it was for him to be able to master the skills of reading / comprehending a long with all the other academic skills which are taught. I had him tested by Sylvan Learning Center his test scores were high in some areas but, in other areas he needed improvement. I enrolled him into Sylvan tutoring program for a year. Besides, that I would still require him to sit with me every day for at least 20 minutes to read out loud to me. Afterwards, we would always have a discussion about what he had read. I wanted to make sure he actually comprehended what it was he was reading and if there was any word he could not pronounce on his own I would hand him the Webster dictionary. I believed in using creative tools to help my son with his reading, and education to keep him focus. Believe it or not it has been truly a journey for me with my son maintaining including keeping him focus on reading and his education being he is one who never liked school from the very first day he attended. What I have shared is only a tip of the iceberg far as me promoting how very important it is to master reading and obtaining a quality education is for one' self. If I had to do it all over again I would not change one signal thing since, I understood and knew the reward at the end of it all.

Qiana Millro, Mother

My reflections about my grandson's education were formulated from a generational concept! My parents expected me to acquire an education. Therefore, I instilled the importance of embracing education into my children, and grandchildren. I paved an educational pathway for my daughter. Hence, my daughter made a path for her son. My daughter and I educationally nurtured my grandson. Our endeavors were successful; until, my daughter's son finished his sophomore year in high school.

My grandson's behavior changed; when, he became a teenager. My grandchild had seemingly become distracted. As a result, my grandson was heading towards destruction. He was on the verge of becoming a black male statistic. In my opinion, some of those distractions surfaced; due to my daughter's absence. Her job had transferred her to South Dakota. Shortly afterwards, my grandson lost his zeal for learning. He was only interested in doing activities with the school's band. Accordingly, his grades reflected his disinterest in academics. My grandson was failing every subject, even P.E.!

The counselor at my grandchild's school suggested an alternative education program for my grandson. The suggested program would allow my grandchild to earn a high school diploma. My daughter and I were interested in the alternative program. Our main objective was for: my grandson to receive a high school diploma. Possessing a high school education is integral in today's society; especially, if you are a black male. It was our desire for our child, and grandchild; to be armed with the tool of a high school diploma. I yearn to teach him how to become: a lifelong learner. Also, he needs discernment.

Young people need the ability to: discern right from wrong. I want my grandson to make good choices in life! The decision to enroll my grandchild in the alternative program marked the beginning of: the rest of his life! First, it severed the "apron strings." Secondly, it detached the "hand holding." My grandchild had stepped into manhood, and he was getting his education! However, secretly I was behind the scenes. I was watching his maneuvers, and decisions. My grandchild was covered with prayers, constantly.

My grandson completed the program's requirements. Now, he is a high school graduate. He is so proud of his accomplishments! I was overwhelmed with joy; because, this meant that my ancestors' prayers were being fulfilled!

Arlinda A. Anderson, B.S.

DEFINITIONS OF KEY TERMS

Hypnosis - Hypnosis is an education communication process to a person's mind that allows the conscious and subconscious mind to come together to get to the same message (IMDHA-2001.)

Intrinsic Factors - include beliefs, morals, and character those things that make up who we are as a person.

Emotional Arousal- Providing emotional arousal while academically performing.

Extrinsic Factors - include environment, other people, and anything outside the body that contributes to change.

Stress - A physical, mental, or emotional reaction resulting from an individual's response to environmental tensions, conflicts, and pressures.

Stressors - environmental factors, intra-, inter, and extra personal in nature, that have potential for disrupting system stability. A stressor is any phenomenon that might penetrate both the flexible and normal lines of defense, resulting in either a positive or a negative factor.

Wellness - wellness is the condition in which all system parts and subparts are in harmony with the whole system of the client.

Stability - The state of balance or harmony requiring energy exchanges as the client adequately copes with stressors to retain, attain, or maintain an optimal level of health thus preserving system integrity.

Performance accomplishments - Successfully winning difficult task with the reward of status or level.

Positive Responses - A good result from an engaged action prompted by a catalyst.

Negative Responses -A negative result from an engaged action prompted by a catalyst.

Verbal Persuasion - Others influencing students self-efficacy through verbal encouragement.

Vicarious Experience - Watching others achieve in a similar area of study as the observer.

Work Habits - Can be viewed as good or bad according to the work environment.

Affect- The observable components of an emotion.

Bright- Happy and Cheerful.

Apathetic- Lack of feeling, emotions, interest or concerns.

Flat- Absence or near absence of any sign of affective expression.

Constricted- Emotions are kept within limits, emotions are limited.

Blunted- A disturbance manifested by severe reduction in the intensity of affect, may respond a little to what is going on.

Labile- Subject to frequent and or unpredictable changes in mood, affect or behavior.

Hostile- Anger and resentment characterized by destructive behavior.

Appropriate- Emotional tone in harmony with accompanying, idea or thought.

Mood- Internal sensations of an emotion.

Euphoric- A false sense of elation or well-being; pathological elevation of mood.

Angry- Feelings of an expression of anxiety that is aroused by a real or perceived threat to one's possessions, values, or significant others.

Irritable- Easily annoyed or provoked; inpatient; fretful.

Sad- Unhappy.

Guarded- Cautions; careful; restraine.

Depressed- Feelings of sadness, despair, unhappiness.

Guilty- Deserving blame or punishment for having committed an offense or having done something wrong.

Cognition- The mental process characterized by knowing, thinking, learning and judging.

Oriented- Conscious awareness of person, place, and time.

Confused- Bewildered, perplexed or unclear.

Thought process- The way a person thinks.

Organized- Logical thoughts.

Concrete- Focused thinking on facts and details, a literal interpretation of messages, and an inability to generate or think abstractly.

Phobic- Persistent fear of an object or a situation.

Paranoid- Suspiciousness which is not based in reality.

Preoccupied- Occupied with or absorbed in one's thoughts.

Disorganized- Confused and/or illogical thoughts.

Loose Association- Thinking in which there is no apparent relationship between thoughts.

Poor concentration- Inability to focus one's thought.

Hallucinations- The occurrence of a sight, sound, touch, smell, or taste without any external stimulus to the corresponding sensory organ; the experience is   real to the person.

Delusional- A false belief which is firmly maintained and is not shared by others and is contradicted.

Illogical- Thinking containing erroneous conclusions or internal contradictions; irrational thoughts.

Tangential- Thoughts veer from main idea and never get back to it.

Self-Harm- Negative consequences for the physical and/or mental well being of oneself.

Ideations- Thoughts.

Hopelessness- A person's belief that neither he nor anyone else can help him.

Self-harm behaviors- An activity that has negative consequences for the person's physical/mental well being.

Aggression- Forceful, verbal and physical action that is the motor counter part of anger, rage or hostility.

Behavior- Any observable, recordable, measurable act, movement or response of a person.

Anxious- Acute feelings that include apprehensiveness, tenseness, fearfulness and feelings of quilt, inadequacy and/or personal worthlessness.

Oppositional- An attitude characterized by ignoring or opposing suggestions of orders from others.

Negative- Lacking in positive quality or character.

Drug-seeking- Asking for medications, especially drugs that have addictive potential.

Agitated- Anxiety associated with severe motor restlessness.

Hyperactive- Restless, aggressive often destructive behavior.

Isolative- Splitting off an emotional component of a thought/emotion, thus avoiding interacting.

Pacing- Walking in a distinctive manner usually with excess anxiety.

Impulsive- A sudden incitement to action without any thought.

Psychomotor Retardation- Marked by slowed speech and body movement.

Withdrawn- Retreat from people or the world by reality.

Waking Hypnosis - A waking suggestion is a suggestion given in the normal state of consciousness which does no precipitate a waking state of hypnosis.

REFERENCES:

Roberts, & White, (1989) - Handbook of Sport Psychology Supports Goal Theory

Almaier, J.(1983, p.4). Comparison of thought-listening rating methods

Fisher, P.F.(1994). Visualization of the reliability in classified remotely sensed

Campbell, D. J., & Stanley, J.C.(1963). Experimental and Quasi-experimental Designs for Research

Collins, A., Joseph, D., & Bielaczyc, K. (2004). Design Research: Theoretical and Methodological Issues. Journal of the Learning Science

Whitman, N. (1985). Student Stress: Effects and Solutions. Retrieved August 7, 2001, form Eric Digest 85-1.

Whitman, Spendlove, & Clark, (1984). Handbook on parenting

Seyle, H. (!976) Stress in Health and Disease. Boston: Butterworths.

Rice, J. (1992) Cultural and other considerations that can influence effectiveness

Ross, S.E., Niebling, B.C., & Heckert, T.M. (1999). Sources of stress among college students. College Student Journal, 33(2), 312-318

Kramer, (1994) Scientific Foundations of Cognitive Theory

Winkler, E.A., (1976). Hypnosis and God

Hewitt, W. (2000) - Simulation Using Adaptive Non-Active Points

Adams, P. (1967) - The New Self-Hypnosis

Winkler, E.A. (1990) - Hypnosis The Key

Winkler, E.A. (1989) p.1 - The Power of Suggestion With Hypnosis

Elman, D.(1964)- Hypnotherapy

Adams, P. (1967) - The New Self-Hypnosis

White, R.W. (1959). Motivation reconsidered. Psychological Review, 60, 599-620

Lepper, M. R. & Malone, Th. W. (1987) Relationships among computer games, fantasy, and learning

Pintrich, P.R. & Schunk, D.H. (2002) Motivation and Learning

Ryan, R.M. & Deci, E.L. 2000 - On happiness and human potentials.. Annual Review of Psychology 52, 141-166

Petri, (1981) - Motivation Theory

Shernoff, Csikszentmihalyi, Schneider, & Shernoff, 2003).

Greeno, J.G. Collins, M. & Resnick, L.B. (1996) A Consideration of Multimedia Instruction

Lepper & Malone, 1987, p.258).Intrinsic Motivation and instructional effectiveness in computer-based education. In R.E. Snow & M. J. Farr (Eds.), Aptitudes, learning and instruction: Cognitive and effective process analysis (Vol.3, pp. 255-287):

Hillsdale, NJ

Deci, E.L., & Ryan, R.M. (1985). Intrinsic motivation and self-determination in human behavior. New York: Plenum.

Wong, D., Perry, S. & Hockenbury, M. (2002). Maternal Child Nursing Care (2nd ed). St. Louis: Mosby

Boyd, M.A. & Nihart, M.A. (1998). Psychiatric Nursing: Contemporary practice. Philadelphia: Lippencott

Wong, D., Perry, S. & Hockenbury, M. (2002). Maternal Child Nursing Care (2nd ed). St. Louis: Mosby

Roth, S., & Cohen, L. J. (1986). Approach, avoidance and coping with stress. American Psychologist, 41(7), 813-819.

Murphy, M.C. & Archer, J.(1996) A qualitative Assessment of personal and academic stressors among college students

Blake & Vandiver, (1988) College students' Academic Stress and Its Relation to their social support

Mattlin, Wethington, & Kessler, (1990) - Contagion of Stress

Seigenthaler, 1997 - Personal needs through leisure activies

Kabanoff &O'Brian,1986 - Terra Linda High School General   Survey

Kaufman, (1988) Assessing adolescent and adult intelligence

Pickens & Kiess,1988Knockout academic stress Via Leisure Reading

Ragheb K.G., & McKinney, J. 1993 -
Satisfaction and fitness act as stress buffers

Tice, D. M., & Baumeister, R.F. (1997). Does
Procrastination and Stress Have An Affect On Your
Health

Ragheb K.G., & McKinney, J. 1993 -
Satisfaction and fitness act as stress buffers

Floyd, J.A. (1991). Nursing students' stress
levels, attitudes toward drugs, and drug use. Archives of
Physic iatric Nursing, 5 (1), 46-53.

Wong, D., Perry, S. & Hockenbury, M. (2002).
Maternal Child Nursing Care (2nd ed). St. Louis: Mosby

Sara, Fine & Ewing, (1999). Family Tree Data

Cordova, D.I., & Lepper, M.R. (1996). Intrinsic
Motivation and the Process of Learning: Beneficial
Effects of Contextualization, Personalization, and
Choice. Journal of Educational Psychology, 88(4), 715-
730.

Graham & Weiner, (1996). Theories and
principles of motivation. In D. Berliner & R Calfee
(Eds.) Handbook of educational psychology (pp. 63-84).
New York: Simon & Schuster Macmillan

Gottfield, A. E. (1985). Academic intrinsic
motivation in elementary and junior high school
students. Journal of Educational Psychology, Vol
77(6)(Dec), 631-645

Lepper, M. R., Corpus, J. H. & Iyengar, S.S.
(2005). Intrinsic and Extrinsic Motivational Orientations
in the Classroom: Age Differences and Academic
Correlates. Journal of Educational Psychology, 97(2),

184-196

Entwisle & Hayduk, (1988) - Children, Schools, and
Inequality

Lynch & Cicchetti, (1997) Theory and method -
Developmental Psychology

Pianta, Steinberg, & Rollins, (1995) Social
Motivation:
Understanding children's school Adjustment

Entwisle & Hayduk, (1988). Children, Schools,
and Inequality

Koschmann, T.D., Myers, A.C., Feltovich, P.J.,&
Barrows, H.S. (1993). Using Technology to Assist in
Realizing Effective Learning and Instruction: A
Principled Approach to the Use of Computers in
Collaborative Learning. Journal of the Learning
Sciences, 3(3),227.

Creswell, J. (2005). Educational Research:
planning, conducting, and evaluating
quantitative and qualitative research (2nd ed.).
New Jersey; Pearson Education.

Cornelius, R.R. (1995). Science of Emotion, The:
Research and Tradition in the Psychology of Emotion.
Upper Saddle River, NJ: Prentice Hall.

Gadamer, H.G. (1977). Philosophical
Hermeneutics. Berkely, CA:
University of California Press.

Warnke, (1987). Gadamer: Hermeneutics,
Tradition, and Reason. Stanford, California: Stanford
University Press.

Tabak, I. (2004). Reconstructing Context:

Negotiating the Tension
    Between Exogenous and Endogenous
Educational Design. Educational Psychologist, 39(4),
225-233.

    Creswell, J. (2005). Educational Research:
    planning, conducting, and evaluating
    quantitative and qualitative research (2nd ed.).
    New Jersey; Pearson Education.

www.ingramcontent.com/pod-product-compliance
Lightning Source LLC
LaVergne TN
LVHW051816080426
835513LV00017B/1979